ABOUT THE AUTHOR

Originally from Brighton, Elle Dillon-Reams has lived in London for
the last 12 years. After dabbling in various poetry nights across the UK,
she won the Genesis Slam in 2019 and is going ahead to the Hammer
and Tongue National Finals at The Royal Albert Hall that was slated
to take place last year. In 2019 she also performed as Boiler House
London's International Women's Day Poet. After winning the Imperial
College Nature Slam in 2020 with her piece FOR FREDDY, she was
then the International Women's Day poet for Imperial College London
in their 2021 celebrations, running a bespoke workshop for doctors,
mathematicians and scientists.

Maladaptive is Elle's first collection of Poetry.

Twitter: @elle_d_reams
Instagram: @elledillonreams

Elle Dillon-Reams
Maladaptive

VERVE
POETRY PRESS
BIRMINGHAM

PUBLISHED BY VERVE POETRY PRESS
https://vervepoetrypress.com
mail@vervepoetrypress.com

FIRST PUBLISHED JAN 2022

Printed and bound in the UK
by ImprintDigital, Exeter

ISBN: 978-1-913917-01-2

Cover image by Lucy Kipper.

CONTENTS

Acknowledgements

Maladaptive

Zwicky 18

Flecks of burning
Irregular
Searching for companion galaxy
Interacting triggers black holes of
Worry
Constellations of conversations on the cusp of
She cuts off her hair, declares ballet is not for this girl
Explosion of potential leaves trail behind
Mum watches through a far away telescope
She is the astronaut of imagination
Daydreams on thumbsucks
Tumble tucks into pools outside of school playgrounds
Pounding feet of older children
Year 6 supernovas who don't know her but show her COOL
Her territory lies in pages of stories, thrust into selecting her
Best Friend
Little cheeks erupt in apology
Flecks burning red
Her mouth clusters of dust

Blush

pink brushed tongue
peony bloom
it's a girl! curled softness
too soon
smooth petals teased open
penetrable
unfurled softness blushed
tongue tied with femininity
in a marshmallow bounce of brevity girl
quiet cry
kiss blown and lost in the wind
little twirling dresses
plumped up pillow teacups
dressups
thumbsucks
pink cancer research badge of 10k
hooray saved the day
she's always ok girl
tied in a neat bow girl
pretty ballet shoes girl
leotard stuck girl
small polite scream girl
hushed.

Disposable Cameras

I used to spend evenings sunburnt and red raw from wax strips
taking off clothes changing clothes hating all clothes
in a fidgety hairy distraction
used to dream of a stolen man-spread with *my* legs stretched
refrain thighs from making out under summer dresses
leaving marks on public seats
swallow down day drinking and anxiety in a still not little enough frame
as bikini beach time chased me
Brighton beach
salty pebbles held
excitement and sweat and hopeful heads
that met to read magazines and discuss teenage dreams
the smell of factor 8 havana oil glistening
on already brown slim friends' bodies
factor 30 thick white cream already left remains
on my denim jean shorts
red pink still sought out my skin
eyes caught squinting
under cheap plastic sunglasses
we notice every male who passes
count the wolf whistles
hold in tummies and secretly miss
the days of our mummies buying us Mr. Whippys
exchanged for rolled up ciggies
we buy vanilla tobacco from the Lanes
there's no replacement for flakes
we take selfies with disposable cameras
to remember
how happy we are

A Better Girl

A better girl.
A better girl is born with a spritz of sweet scented perfume
No shit nor blood down her back but sparkles of sequins
No roar nor feral scream from her
A better girl soprano sings when she cries
She immediately likes pink
She immediately LOVES pink
A better girl is sugar and spice and all things nice
She is so NICE
This girl is a ballerina
This girl is a perfect pirouette
This girl is dainty and small and petite
This girl 'smiles love'
This girl hopes it might never happen
This girl isn't just wolf whistles
This girl is woodland creatures
and songbird serenades wherever she walks
This girl doesn't walk, she
Floats
She glides
Such pride in her purity
This girl is forever virginal
This girl is thin and white and blemish free and ALWAYS HAPPY
This girl never drinks beer
This girl has the occasional sip of a white wine spritzer through
  an eco conscious straw

This girl is perfect

This girl smiles love hopes it might never happen love
This girl has NO HAIR ON HER BODY BELOW HER EYELASHES
This girl is a perfect size 8 or 6 we can't say size zero anymore
This girl is not a size zero but slimmmm
with a demure amount of boob or bottom
This girl is well spoken and intelligent but not too intelligent
This girl is blowdry bliss
I woke up like this
The girl won't kiss on a first date
This girl makes the boys wait
BUT SHE ISN'T FRIGID
This girl gets married and has 2.5 kids and her vagina stays e x a c t l y
the same
This girl is a cook and cleaner and a mother and routinely offers the
perfect blowjob and does it all in 6 INCH STILETTO HEELS
This girl feels great all the time really fine
This girl honestly doesn't mind
THIS GIRL IS SO HAPPY

Flowers For My Mother

whose stems clenched tight in sweaty fist of hopeful
optimism kills
colourful buds bloomed too soon

whose petals are pulled like ponytails too tight
the rest wilts under the strain of being smaller smaller
smaller
whose pollen she's allergic to
just suddenly
just today

whose pollen I spiked with sullen sadness and heartbreak that she's
not who she used to be
whose insides are bruised after force opening petals
when the winter was still too cold
whose wrapped bouquet decoration is ripped
whose smell delighted the bees
delighted the others and she
wrote a tweet about daughters needing better boundaries

flowers that are too expensive and too complicated to choose to buy
but still ones I try to give her
cos I owe her that much

Flowers for my mother

whose stems clenched tight in sweaty fist of hopeful
optimism killed
colourful buds
bloomed too soon

Patriarchal Obedience

Can you be smaller
Can you shrink
Can you be quieter
You are too much
Too much
Too much
Fold up conveniently please
With ease
Do not cause fuss
Do not make noise
Keep poised
Quietly
If you're going to speak
Shut the door
Silently
No more loudness
Greatness
Big ness
Just small
Say please
Say sorry
You are too much
Rub your edges out discreetly
And neatly
Softer quieter
Completely beige
No offensive colour nor sound
You don't need to be found
Just fade into the background

Shh
No sounds
My dear
If you could disappear that would be
Neater
Cleaner
Easier and nicer
Now
Please shush into invisibility
You are too much
You are not enough

Sorry.

Home

straight train line down the tracks
grid from station and corner and up hill
and uphill and up hill and up hill and up
Up Up and away
I worry I used to be fitter
a wave cresting with excitement Home
crashing with anxiety Home
will they still remember me Home
I'm not who I used to be Home
hoping it's better now Home
hoping we'll be together now Home
last night I didn't get to sleep at all
thread the tethers frayed between fingers
breaking at the phone rushes
in stops and starts she's always late
she breaks suddenly feels frantically at the
pockets and pockets eyes
bursting out of sockets flitting for the train
platform confirmation despite
the fact at this station
it's always the same
draws ticket from her side like a sword and charges
forward
runs bleeps
runs weeps
tries to let the sunshine in
chugging jolts shunts then properly begins
sits on the moving forward motion and regresses
like she's going backwards

backpack held close to chest
an hour of rest then pounds feet up a hill
damp armpits and back from a rucksack too full
a knock and a pause
she waits unsure
wonders what she came here for
one less bell to answer
increases awareness
though won't ever meet that awareness head on
she always worried in this shape
she doesn't quite belong stuck
to the grid but doesn't realise
she's 4 or 5 dimensions away from their song

Shiny Happy People

I'm good at being glittery
the life and soul of the party I used to feel
heavy shame guilty when I couldn't be Shiny
even littlest me recognised quickly
it is better to be Happy
people like you Shiny and Happy
people are magpies
and the shame that came from feeling matte
spat smiles out of wobbly teeth mouths
sour from swallowing down sad
sometimes everything is wrong
sure I'd had enough
Shiny Happiness gone
sad called your bluff dragged me
down to the depths
down to the darkness
they all warned would be a lonely place
but heard another face singing a different song
another soul struggled through days too long
a call to hang on
a revolutional truth
smacked me round the face
like an aggressive sudden wisdom
tooth
now there was reassurance Everybody Hurts
the night is yours alone
no not just me
Everybody Hurts
a reminder to hang on

in a tuneful melody it was ok to sing along
hold on
sometimes everything is wrong
hold on
but now it's time to sing along
hold on
When your day is long

Hold on. Hold on. Hold on.

Footwear

Growing out of your favourite sparkly shoes
Toes crunch and curl please I still want to be that girl
Unwillingly unfurled
Proved the fit is no longer appropriate
So get rid
But I wanted to dance twinkle-toed fancy free
Not ready to give up that version of me
Pretty
Pleasing
Ever so appealing
What now
Sensitive soles
Gravel crunching under bare feet lost
Blistered and raw
Swollen and sore
Hard skin grows protective
Toes explore and find space to take up
that isn't dainty
nor delicate
They stomp
They strut
Then what
My next pair were a pair of sturdy Doctor Martens
I tied in double knots

Pancakes

And then there was the 3am we've been instant messaging all
   night and he says we should meet

and I have had just enough vodka and cranberry *and tequila*
   and handing me my cloak room ticket and coat back

the attendant catches my drunken eye and winks

and I think of nothing else than

going home alone isn't going home alone

if I've got my phone and he's messaging

and he's saying I'm sweet we should meet

and I press the largest fuck it button tinder has to offer and tell
   him to come over

I don't sober up until he's inside me

he is rough

and I wonder why men think its a good idea to grab your
throat whilst fucking you

and I wonder why I don't tell him to stop

some days I want to stop

press Bernard's watch

pause

and go for a swim in the stillest waters I can find

Fish absent

People absent

spend a whole day on a holiday from time

only thinking of the needs that are mine

his spine is sweaty

and the vertebrae scowl at me

he howls as he

flips me over like a

pancake days in our house were never that fun cos I never
    liked batter

my siblings would say it doesn't matter it's all about the toppings

popping more and more sugar and lemon and cream and
    grateful grins dripping slivers of golden syrup shine

My spine shouts at me to say stop

I bite my lip

he thinks its kinky

my teeth betray me and keep howls prisoner

I don't sleep

The next morning I pretended I had work

got dressed put on makeup told him I needed to leave

he said he'd walk me to the tube

so I pretended I'd left my oyster at home

'you go ahead'

he kissed me goodbye said he'd text

I bit my lip again to stop my mouth from betraying me once again

and beginning to cry

Some days I want to find him

I want to scratch out his starved eyes

tear out his urgent impolite tongue

and gut him like a pig.

Pit

the floor was lava and now burnt cinders
blackened lifeless
it makes the room smell of smoke and ash and death
sooty soles of feet shouldn't slip
under sheets clean with red and yellow
but the soap wouldn't take away the stain of mourning
my floor is sad
carpets could not stay under such a wave
the big black dog left his mark
tattooing every floorboard and rotting the timber I walk on
when I used to get out of bed
now my body is as lifeless as the lacking coloured floor
underneath me
I stay wrapped in sheets of red
my soles sooty
my head a mess

Dandelion

Nothing will grow here
burnt cinders of remorse
ash settled like snowflakes
crumbled in fingertips burnt
so the sensitivity is lessened in touch

Nothing will grow here
naïve seeds sewn in regret
a false optimism of promise
it's too late
blind nose searches for a root
upturns the corpses
fabric lilies decorated her plastic headstone

Nothing will grow here
a rude bud pushes out of the burial
initially dismissed
she is hope

No Is A Safehouse

I want to make a safehouse for the girl whose mouth wouldn't
   make the shape of no
Didn't have the strength to howl loud enough back
Didn't have the strength to superhero fly kick
Crash
      Bang
          Wallop
              Whack
Bubble shield rebound
Hungry hands pound the ground instead of pulling away at
Layers of shirt tucked in
Buttons ripped
Underwear pink
Seams slip
Layers of skin
Ponytail gripped
She is not an onion
Dirty fingernails are permitted to peel
Sour tears leak as a way of protest
then turn to acid under the touch of intruders pillaging
Burn away
No.
She doesn't cry this time but breathes fire and roars
                                   NO
And No is a vomit hurl forward of destruction
No is an inferno blaze catapulting claws from stolen body in
   abduction
No is a white heat battle blaze deconstruction of predatory
   body from violent mind

Blinded by fire
Burnt to cinders and inhaled by every other male who dared to
   stare grab what they wrongfully assumed was theirs
Roar unadulterated howls of a sewn tight together mouth
   ripping out stapled shut sensibilities with an outpour
No more
No is a safe house
No is the first word girls should have been taught to shout

Where Are The Other Allies?

If you put your pants over your tights, you look like a superhero.
I know how to make a Zorro mask out of a pillowcase
Bouldering and rock climbing can have the effects of spidey senses
If you parkour over fences and stand proud with your hands on
your hips, just make sure your cape doesn't get stuck, else it'll rip.
If you put your keys between your fingers, you look and feel like
Wolverine.

Try not to be seen, keep your head up, walk confidently.
Have your headphones on, but your theme music turned low, just
    so you know if anyone's walking behind you.
Don't make eye contact.
But clock the publicly lit spaces in case of villain chases
Clock the exits and count them
One, two, three,
For perfecting your Wolverine growl is important and gives you
    more time to escape
The boys in blue wont do anything to help
So maybe try waving a bus down?
And if you're going to make a sound, shout 'Fire'
People are much more likely to come for fire than-
Remember not all heroes wear capes.

To the woman who became my cape
Who knew without either of us saying anything that he
After eyeballing me, was ready to be

STOP. Please Stop.
I'm actually meeting someone you see

So it's really not ok for you to be so,
Sit so close
No thankyou
No sorry, I

His eyes to my face, chest, thigh
STOP. And the woman takes stock
Bolts upwards
Wishing he'd leave, she grabs security
He leans in closer
'Excuse me sir'
He scowls at me.
Eyes burn into mine for what seems like far too long a time

But this time, he does leave
Eventually.
I breathe,
Look at the woman, mouth 'Thankyou'
and she brushes it off as if it were nothing
As if it were the nothing I wished his intentions were
As if it were the nothing everyone else around her who bore
    witness did
An acceptable composure regained as fear and panic hid
Threat dispersed
Knowing full well it could have been
and has been worse.

Where are the other allies?

Those quietly active like the woman who helped
and those loudly roaring
Soaring through the sky

Who cry when we cry
Who howl when we howl
Who refuse to throw in the towel
Who know that yes hashtags can help
But being there physically when we are afraid to
yelp
Is the real superheroes role

So let's aim, let's make a shared goal
To get up, stand up,
Refuse point blank to shut up if we see those in need
Refuse point blank to tire if we see those being thrown into
the fire
BE those Heroes
Who are the pants over your tights reassuring you
You'll be alright
You are seen

So that one day we don't
have to teach them to hold keys between their
fingers like Wolverine.

For Freddy

Stones under bare feet, pebbles round, hard,

The smell of salt

It was only a dare

Splash

He dived in after him

Splash

Wasn't scared

Splash

Rough waves

Constant waves, constant in and out in and out waves, foam spray off the top of waves,

Crashing waves, drowning waves

Pouring, wet, cold, fresh,

Engorged seaweed grabs ankles,

Wraps around little legs,

Tickles legs weightless,

All legs seem little here

Roar of white horses

Wind moans

Pebbles are stone

Pebbles are home

Soles of feet didn't have time to get hard this summer

Caw of gulls up ahead,

Laughter of children,

I've got older now

Laughter of gulls

They've got bolder now

Steal sandwiches from toddlers now

Remember when 99s were 99p?

Approximately 5000 items of beached marine plastic pollution

Bigger hand squeezes little hand at sight of ice cream van

Per mile of beach in the UK

Falling over promises green

Mint choc chip

Pulled under into silence,

Pressure on head numbing out all sound in a calm violence

Beating chest

Weightless

Salt stung lips

Roly poly hold your nose

Mermaid strength to pull up breathe out

With waves that are feral horses bucking

Don't get cocky

Surrender to the surge

Rise purges everything forth eventually

Salt from the sea always gave the nicest curls to beachy hair
without a care

It was only a dare

He dived in after him

Wasn't scared

No fear

Didn't intend to reach hero status

Premature end

Attempts to mend body found 4 miles out from the pier

That's approximately 20,000 items of beached marine plastic
pollution away

They say he wasn't scared

No fear

Hand holding

Gulls cawing

Waves crashing

Disbelief thrashing

We're meant to be invincible in our twenties.

Plenty of seasides still to see

Plenty of paddles rolled up trousers to the knee

Plenty of lick your salt covered ice cream smothered lips in
  unadulterated glee

Plenty of sunsets

Though no amount guaranteed

His was the first non religious funeral I ever attended.

The sound of the waves is still one that calms me

And I feel guilty

I'm so much older than you'll ever be.

Grandad

wearing a dress I was worried I might look fat in
down the residential street
some of my cousins and I hadn't seen each other since the last
    funeral
last time we saw an empty can of strawberry daiquiri with a plastic
    straw on the pavement
I had sweaty palms
I wait for the traffic lights
clenched tight the speech I was meant to read because I'm
    good at reading and I read for a job and I read out loud to
    large groups of people for a job and I promised I wouldn't cry
swan boats for tourists
but my throat closed up and let me down
drowned out sound
the canals
sobbed my way through the words
me and lisa stood with the 4 men
on one side a crossfit always open
hold the coffin
on the other side a GAMMON pub
lisa is a bodybuilder
we are the first female pallbearers our family has ever seen
under the tunnel and up past the wild flowers that grow
next to he was heavier than I thought he'd be
loud traffic
but the act
the physical act
the birds I don't know the names of

stopped me crying
the vicar instructed us to lower him down into the grave
over the bridge to the babies
we'd never practised
the moorhens and cygnets and ducklings
I worried we'd drop him
I worried I shouldn't smile when the vicar congratulated us
    on being strong I worried I'd laugh out of the Richard Curtis
    absurdity of it all
and the terrapin I've seen twice but no one else has I wonder if it
really exists

Kintsugi

thin skin stretched over a universe
limpid, revealing
black holes and supernovas burning too gold too bright it
hurts eyes
thin skin sheer hidden mistakes, destitute damage inside
translucency leaks it all
too visible
I tried
brain break mental health break lets
take 5 it's important to focus fuck off
sorry
mistake
I'd like to take a break have a break
have a 106 calorie kit kat
bones snap, facade crack, snap
back, stuck together with blu tac,
out of whack, first aid pack, plaster can't
fix, smile tricks, eyelid flick, chest kicks
out breath stuttered I'd like a break
muttered through voice shake voice quake
thin skin butter fingers slip glass smash
leaked soul ash
bad sleeper
thin skin crystalline
so the gold fills deeper, fills sweeter,
fills aches and keeps her
alight
gold joinery though feeling pointless

she in recovery
backed herself pointedly
embracing flaws, sore imperfections pour
over creatively
stars twinkly bring a torch to see a more
beautiful art leads her to be
a stronger galaxy

Hovis

I haven't eaten bread in 5 years

because the fear of carb consumption hurt more than the hunger pangs

because of the indigestion already bringing up bile from the diet culture

because puppy fat isn't acceptable after you turn 15

because the bulge in my leotard pulled me to the back of the ballet barre

because the bulge in my leotard pulled my chin down to the plied feet

because the bulge in my leotard was the butt of your joke

because the effort you went to in making loaves rise would never elevate the downtrodden insecurity

because nothing tastes as good as skinny feels

because ATKINS

because thigh gap because size zero

because one slice was the apple on the tree of the garden of Eden and I was not bold enough to be Eve

because I would rather faint than not fit in
because that was the dress size I so desperately wanted to fit in

because 'you're not thin or pretty enough to play a lead role'
 was a tenet passed by authority

because amongst bicarb of soda, laxatives, and toilet paper,
 there was no room left for the bread to fit in

because I feigned intolerance

because I feigned fullness

because I was all too good at distracting away from my mouth
 and that crust

because I was scared

because nothing tastes as good as skinny feels was tattooed on
 my taste buds from the age of 8

because relentless self punishment left no time for buttered
 toast

Sunday On The Central Line

The shrieks precede their entrance.
Shudders from nearby bodies
realising their sentence.
Wondering what crime they committed
to deserve this painful penance.

Wheels screech to a halt.
The revolt begins
with an assault on quivering ears.
Peering up from phones and books
swallowing down a moan.
Internal appeals.
Drowned by the sound of
tottering heels.

Get on the next carriage,
get on the next carriage.
Smells of gin tin cans
prosecco perfume
and impending marriage.

No hiding me,
no hiding we.
The bride to be exclaims
Oi Behave yourself!

The others giggle in glee
at this authority
squawk almost parental.
She is the sergeant general.
Leading her battalion
of blow-dried hair
onto the central line.
Conducting them with
an inflatable penis
and a bottle of sparkling wine.

No one shows they mind
until the man sitting next to me
feels a sudden arrival
of pink feather boa
adorned pickled little body.
Presented she of the bridal party:

I wanna go wee!
She whines
I can't hold it all that time!

The man in black next to me
seems to be wincing
and internally rinsing
his hands in anxiety
Why won't she get off me?

We all sympathise
but its best in situations such as these
to avert one's eyes.

The surprise arrival of hen
onto his lap
makes the others cackle,
cheer, and clap

OMG Kayleigh you're such a tart!

Don't make me laugh or I'm gonna fart!

The man cringes further
in extreme unease.
Mutters under his breath
get off me please

Kayleigh is pulled off
like a team game of tug of rope
We're off in two stops!
The tube breathes into a sense of hope.

They quieten gradually.
Within the group
are three generations of family
Each one as pickled as the other.
The Lambrini bottle is passed to grandmother
who wears a headband of
penis deely-boppers.

Swigging down fizz
integral for hen-hydration
Their volume increases
As they get close to

the final destination.
They topple after tipples
too many to count.
Precision required
To mount the platform...

There's a shared smile as doors slide back
into silent closed preference.
A sense of pride at endurance.
A smile which quickly fades.
All safe in the assurance
that no further communication
between passengers is required.
No need for public protocol
to be rewired.

Back to your individual books,
your individual phones.
Back to silent bubbles of quiet
for the rest of your way home.

Driver Eyeballs Through The Back Mirror To Look At A Kind Man's Face

A man's kind face
who forgot his headphones
no safe cocoon to keep him alone with his thoughts
He's forced to reply

Hi

Driver questions why this country's gone to shit
5 seconds into the door opening, Kind Man sits
releasing this won't be a comfortable flit from home to work
His bones moan, shirking from this attempt at debate but
too late
It's a 40 minute journey.
Not wanting to be surly, he smiles politely

I know,
      Mate.

An attempt at casual friendship,
An attempt to get off the hook for this guilt he so constantly feels,
An attempt to find unity.
Kind Face Man prays he's not at the behest of lunacy,
slips his phone into his pocket as Driver says

We've lost all sense of community
Lack of opportunity for the youth
seems to me they want us out of this country

But they don't see
My kids, my family was raised here, it's clear they're more London than
'other'

Kind Face Man sees a fight between eyes and tears trying to escape

The shape of things to come
Frightens me.

Kind Face Man swallows silently and wishes violently he had the
right words to say

Take my son for example
He's into football
That's all
I wish he was better at school but it's cool he's no fool
He's got dreams
Plays on the best team for his year and wants to play for England in the
world cup

He chokes up
Rolls up sleeves as if that could roll up the toxic masculinity that
howls he shouldn't
Be doing this.

My son doesn't have no fear
About not being allowed to.
But the current climate of crowd would hound you for daring to break
rank, we don't engage
Disconnected, disenfranchised, and enraged
We stare at screens so we don't have to see Mother Nature howl
Scowl at headlines

Aching spines
Hearts pine for something more.

We pour drink after drink and sink lower into another weekend
    overdraft spend How come all my friends are happier than me?
/Wealthier than me
/Prettier than me
/Snappier than me
/Slimmer than me
/Fitter than me
/Trimmer than me
My son doesn't see. Doesn't have any of that yet.
I don't know how to burst his bubble
Pop his dreams.
What if they tell him he can't because he doesn't seem
British enough?

Kind Face Man wants to smooth this rough, make cheery,
    make clean. It doesn't seem fair.
And he does care.
He swallows down regrets that rise to the surface like acid
    reflux
Regrets that he's not in charity, or politics, or human rights
His destination is in sight, he knows this interaction, this
    interlude, not meaning to be rude, is coming to an end,
And in reality, they're just two strangers.
A worker providing a service.
Far from confidable friends.

The taxi takes a sharp bend and he feels a pull greater than the
    awkwardness choking him from a seatbelt to stay in place.
He can't fix his privilege, can't change his race.

Eyes flit out the window longing for air and space
Driver pulls to a stop and wipes damp eyes and nose
Kind Face Man's guilt grows,
He shows a sympathetic smile,
Throws his seatbelt back
Grabs important rucksack and,
Feeling strange,
Gets out a twenty
and a ten

Here,
      Mate.
Keep the change.

We Are London

We are London
We are rented accommodation house
Swiping hungry fingers to find a spouse
We are the blackened tube mouse
Tailless but full of stories
Will spare the gory details
Never fails to entertain
Self deprecated decorated fables of fine
Comedy supports our spine
It's better if we claim we don't mind
But It's Fine.

We are London
We are weary heads falling
Into graffitied glass panes on endless
Commutes home
Bones rusting and in need of more than just a spring clean
    dusting
Nodding off and entrusting we'll wake up
Before the last stop
We are another Tinder date disaster flop
Popping into Tesco express on our way back
Starving for another's touch
A snack more than this £3 meal deal for dinner we
Wished was just a one time thing
Crack open a can of fizzy tranquilizing enticement
Getting ID'd brings excitement
Until you realise you lost your drivers licence in some Ketamine
    club land environment

Getting violent in passive aggressive rage
Cos some button tight shop assistant don't believe your age
Stuck in a cage where it initially felt like flattery to look
Younger than you actually are
Doesn't get you far
When this explosion of come on mate mouth
Stuck with sedentary swear words and cigarette tar.
Starting to spar fists are charged
Brow knits hard
Barge through this fog of toxic masculinity writ large
But It's Fine.

We are London
We are shipwrecked souls
In a murky Thames sea of lost hope floating goals
We are mindless scrolls
Scanning Twitter trolls
Skinny teas to omit soft rolls
Of bodily waves
Caving into grave scapegoat triggering headlines
Prisoners to deadlines and parking fines
Celebrity shrines and fading hairlines
We are online Shrinking waistlines
Keeping up to date on Palestine so long our finger flick petition
    click doesn't trick us further under the poverty line
We need to realign this percentage sign
Its diagonal grinds us time after time under a ceiling of glass
We seemingly can't be arsed
But It's Fine.

We are London

We are major capital city
Unrelenting state of feeling shitty
Gritted teeth
Ribs underneath paper thin skin long to be wings
Heart longs to sing
More than this swan song
How did it all go so wrong?
We are starving for another's touch
Caffeinated sugared alcoholic crutch
Holding up yearning pipe dream aspirations
Figuring as such
That to be fine

It's best if you don't hope for much.

We are London
We are fed on capitalism and shifting attainable prisms
Except knowing the constant ism that
Sex sells
We pull at rejected flesh and itch our lower ribbed scar
Newly lain for Grenfell
Not every death reported in the headlines
We are a circus we tightrope walk the breadline
Fine Tuned to this clear austerity
We are stinging sore city
And ain't it a pity
That we have the capacity for change
To change
But strange enough
When life gets tough
Feeling rough leads you to close eyes down
Focus on individual reasons to frown

We are London town
A wasteland of wasted souls and broken hearts

So I make this art
In some helpless way
I hope it makes it just a bit more ok.

Mollusc

Sometimes when the gremlins get really loud I shut down
neglecting all human contact or interaction as gremlins go
burrowing into my skin making it itch with worry.
The first time I tried to see if I could avoid eye contact with
anyone all day the morning was easy
Generally no human eyes are necessary when our phones can
provide without pleasantries far more stimulation
At each station I'd avert my gaze just to make sure
New passengers wouldn't acknowledge me as they passed
    through the doors
The floor I studied
noticed the speckled grey pattern shine
Looked at the smart business brogues compared to rough split
    converse mine
When one became spare I wasn't offered a seat,
I think they are exclusively reserved for those who are neat I
    can't compete
Not me in my leggings and aging rucksack
Overfilled bursting at the seams at my inability to pack.
Light.
Ever.
But here you just can't tell with the weather
So to be clever I take pleasure in taking never only one layer
    but several options
just in case
A plethora of choice. Almost miss my stop-
I rush off and think about reserving not only eyes but voice.
I won't speak I won't communicate
just for curiosity to see if I can

A ban on connection.
All at once a sudden impact-
An aggressive shove as they walked past
But not me nor any other person said anything or looked
Perhaps I'm invisible at last
I go to the ticket barrier and my oyster won't let me through
What to do?
But I'm quickly bleeped in without a single word nor
acknowledgement by a man dressed in blue
There's a sense of relief... few
It's now a challenge and thrill
To see how long I can last and survive
Nil by eyes
Nil by mouth making words
Nil by connection and it's a surprise
You can disappear quite easily here
Invisibility isn't something that requires positivity nor agility
I'm slow
Against the commuters I'm flotsam and jetsam
Low in importance and low in care
They don't stare
I'm barely there.

When I come back into focus
the gremlins hushed not completely but just enough so I can
function
My skin feels raw, soft

punctured, and penetrated
burnt and sensitive
No shell left.
A mollusc.

Little Buttercup

boldest print flower
curled edges of grandeur
yellowing cleavage of creases
leathering under red petals pinched in rouge
enticing touch
brown ruffled hills
oozing distorted smiles of horizons
straighter than straight too straight
from trying to show all their teeth
underneath pockets of glitter
that never degraded never faded
sparkle as they may they don't take away
the smell of shit sticks to you
clings to fingertips
closer now than the loneliness baby wipes
could not rub away
it is fetid
the carpet weeps with each foot step
leaves a residue that you can never quite wipe away
yellow sticker reduced wallpaper
achingly peels off ill fitting walls
moaning creaking floorboards
the furniture is winging again
shh warm cuddle,
nestle out of the sofa and into my chest nuzzle
chin on top of my head snug,
safe swaddled in cuddle
smile and sigh and slow down and stroke back safe

it's ok now
I've got you now
don't worry now
slow down and warm up in softness
little butter cup
stroked cloak of light brown smoke
comforting unassuming
not at all confusing
in cushioned spaces
in soft warm spaces
traces left over your faces

Bridge

after Caroline Bird

this Bridge is up up high, we were warned not to look down
lest we got scared, lest we lose our footing, lest we slip and fall,
you started rocking it from side to side and the rope burned
on my palms, I wish I stayed on the other side

no, this Bridge is made of broken beer bottles, some blue when
you promised you'd stop drinking, I pretended not to notice
the vodka woven between promises of sober shards of sorry
made my eyes bloodshot tinted rose

no, this Bridge is made of bruises and broken fingers broken
promises, this Bridge is one I was thrown down the stairs onto,
pushed up against the railings, this bridge was carved out of
Jekyll and Hyde and even though it whimpers when you raise a
fist this bridge is stronger than even the concept of a list poem

no, this Bridge is made of all the cliches of 'As Long As He
Needs Me' and toxic masculinity, this Bridge tried to grab my
kicking feet as I leapt off into the unknown, this Bridge is a
manipulative memory,
but this Bridge is just a memory

the ones I tread on now, have Poohsticks thrown from them
and running water underneath them,
regardless of stumble trips,
I feel my feet grounded on sturdier foundations.

Salad Cramps

A woman taps me on the shoulder
In Holland and Barrett
Alarmed
Masked strangers whisper whisper to one another
We look like spies
The staff hold breaths
Look on with wide
Red grapefruit Eyes
Me there for a small health allowed chocolate *alternative*
to satisfy a heavy
                Heavy
                    period.
I'd found Salad
Cramps these last few days
flooring
Though no pain allows for the actual
Dairy Milk
Bag full of veg from Sainsbury's
Headphones full of Green veg Guilty Feminist podcast
She taps
I turn
She whispers in ear
Still encased in headphone
I say
        What?
Before I realise
I have to take the headphones off to hear her whispered tones
She repeats

in soft discreet hushed

You have *some... thing....* On your trousers...

And gives me the look,

That look echoed by the sympathetic smile friend stood
  behind her

Hiya

That *some... thing*

I know instantly what

Pull of my jumper quickly

I'm not hot

And tie it round my waist in the GUILT FREE snack aisle

Blushing

But grateful for my I'veJustBeenForARun outerwear

that compliments and covers up this red face embarrassed
  shade of shame

I pretend to scan the snacks

For 1, 2, 3

                        Then leave

clenching

myself

together

Full of RED

Full of gratitude for that woman

For that sister

Who understood

Who reached out

I whisper   *Thankyou for telling me*

back into her ear

And walk out head bowed

In grief for the ignorant naïve pre-bleed me

On Hands

Everyone hold Hands
Cos you can tell a lot about a woman by her hands
For instance
If they're round your neck
It probably means she's upset

I'll hold my own hand
With its 12 little freckles
The skin is older now than it used to be
I don't wear hand cream
A scar on the centre of wrist
But you can tell a lot about a person By their hands
For instance
Long fingers piano-player's hands
Anxiety means they're often clammy
Palms are sweaty
My piano teacher used to get out a
Special wipe Tea wipe Towel
When I had lessons
And it was meant to make it ok
But I winced with shame
Knees weak
When she wiped the keys,
Wiped the moisture away

Wiped clammy palms
Arms are heavy
Apologies spilled down chin already

Mom's spaghetti
Not really, we had veggie burgers for dinner.

The index finger more sensitive than the rest
Scarred from a hand blender I slipped with
Too many cuts to stitch with
I was making protein balls to shrink myself thin with
They glued it back together
scars nobbly
Knuckles nobbly
I probably should wear hand cream

You can tell a lot about a person by their hands
This one broke
When he clenched fists hit
He pushed me down the stairs it's your fault bitch
He'd casually spoken
The hospital said it's broken
But there was nothing they could do
No glue this time
So I made a splint out of a lolly stick
I had to eat the lolly first to get the lolly stick
It was a Solero
It made me feel a bit sick

But you can tell a lot about a person by their hand shakes
Right now we still cannot handshake strangers
And I'm glad
Strangers often wince wipe
Read too much into it wipe
We wash these palms and backs of hands for 20 seconds
Frequently

We antibac and wear gloves and try not to imagine the germs
Breading vividly whilst soap singing Happy Birthday
Untouched hands raw with sanitising

I prefer the rawness
Because you can tell a lot about a person by their hands

Maybe my palms sweat
Because the worry needs somewhere to go
Wipe
This is why I don't wear hand cream
This is why fountain pens for handwriting
Were always a nightmare at school
Children can be cruel and when you grow up
With people saying
urrr what's wrong with you
You wipe hands down school jumpers and try not to cry

I have a condition called hyperhidrosis
I'm writing about it in case it helps someone else
Accept their thing that makes them different
Sometimes it's nice not to have to
Hold your own hand isn't it?
These are my hands
I accept them as ok largely
Palms are sweaty, knees weak
Mine are sparkly.

January

The sunlight today was missing
she hid behind swathes of mist and fog
disguised
had a bad case of the mondays
created horror fantasy scenes
from an agatha christie
ever so dramatic
watch our breath go up into the sky
without a care
softer lighting means the bags under
eyes are less frightening
I still hide self view so I only see you
it's easier to focus
feel happy the whole way through
we walked through the park
through the branches dividing ours
and the next door neighbours
the opposite block of council flats
stark blocks of anbaric light
bright
there are only three flights of stairs in ours
in theirs they have 10
warms cold toes wiggling
thick outdoor adventurer socks
and the light pollution from the sky
from the lampposts high nearby
on the main road where the cars go
stop us from seeing stars in the night sky

we watch flames dance and die
and smile
the smell left in our hair from the
bonfire air I've always preferred the
morning light
uninterrupted
sunrise over the highrise
the glow
of potential and possibility
predictably the light brings back
the state of lived in
workspace/living-room/office space
discarded layers christmas hats
splayed
across yesterday's festivities left
lonesome on sofas neglected by
mondays
the cat doesn't seem to mind
finds joy in being spoiled for choice in soft
furnishings
as we busy ourselves with things like laptops
and sensible working spots chairs
for backs made to sit sober and still
the sunlight was missing today
took absence of leave with the weekend's
dopamine still we gazed out windows and
wondered where she could be

House Red Please

You blushing claret
smooth softening and slowing
flowing warmth
that made young tastebuds wince
the £3 insulter we chugged with a can of Dr
Pepper before a gig
now upgraded *(to at least a fiver)*
strokes down older throats in gloats of what
wisdom age gives taste

You are smooth jazz
complemented by glass
coped with in mugs
plastic cups suffice
You are the very bestest vice
glug
       glug
              glug
sipped rich it kisses
rosy cheeked witty
quips leisurely embraced
with dark velvet touch

You nocturnal quiet
softener of rat race riot
intelligent heat smooths a heady beat
rubs your feet
thaws wounds

You are an open fire in bloom
The world outside paused
just for a bit
You are cheers!
to laughs
to tears
to sharing the momentous
and the ordinary
the average and nothing much,
the slowing the embracing
of another week day evening
And still a refined tipple of
choice

You gentle coaxer of stilted voice
let's get the bottle
as we burrow in for the
night

I'm here to listen
a stressor blur
a subtle slurrr of words
glug
      glug
            glug
and still
a glass with a film transforms
you into that plush grownup
you hoped you might one day
be
You friend warmer stranger
bonder

bad date soother softening
groover
You are 2 for £10
and still seem fancy

You lockdown easer
fluent burgundy
Oh how I love thee
In this anything but dry
January.

Mothballed

on hold

hard acerbic wail

pail of sour milk too long

long kept

train that crept rudely

into extreme unexplained delay

broken toilets

crackled apologies for endless inconvenience

absurd diversions no heating

the snack trolley solely stocked with stale ham sandwiches

and they're £20

and you in this beige box carpeted walls enclosure

on hold to offbeat and slightly flat

predictably

start to spike heavy into a hormonal walrus

quiet violence turning into an all encompassing virus

complaint

after complaint

after complaint

after complaint

shit stain stuck to soles of shoes

the harassment of boredom

diarrhoea on a romantic date

sludge mud envelopes optimism

a prison of tax returns

grey greeeey liminal space

on hold

on hold

still on hold

hold on

The Expectancy Of Utopia

the hubbub of multi-people unmuted

celebrating

the crying with laughter

the crying with release

the jokes

the tangents on tangents on tangents

of conversation

the bleary eyed smiles wide

the smelling of each other's otherness

the shampoo the perfume the aftershave

the youness

touch

we hold hands across table brush legs

arms wraps around who's next to who

on a shared elongated bench

the mad hatters tea party swap seats

and the sharing try this share mine

oh that's delicious I knew you'd love it too

time unfurls gently

peacefully

the sun warms the captivity away

and we're ok

and then the free flowing wine slurs

us out of listening and now everyone is insisting

they're the most important point of view

and you

sat across the table all lipstick smeared teeth

and the disapproval

re-establishing itself as the novelty dies with the sunset

the nagging worry fret fumbles

out of a misshapen mouth

distance didn't make our hearts grow fonder

test failed

the grateful tears turn to wails

babies wanting someone to take them home again

Stockholm Syndrome roams around bold

we cry for them to lock us up again.

After The End

This life came with no manual

No toolkit to fix when problems prove tangible

No off switch to reset to restart to re begin

As much as glitter powders potions and pills numb from the out

all the way in

Their fixability and mending capabilities are thin

You can't paint your skin with makeup to make up the problems from within

My core rotten and forgotten

I lost sight of little me

The little she with dreams so very big of the things that she could be

The little girl who could have conquered the whole wide world

Still could

Still should

Attempt to try anyway

Life's too precious to waste another day

Wishing I was someone else or better something gone and not here

Burning skin in showers too hot and wishing I could disappear

It's not clear, it's not easy, I don't think it ever will be

There are still days when I cannot find the sun

A sense of empty's not how it's meant to be

Your twenties don't have to be tidy

You are a beautiful patchwork quilt of plenty

With mended stitched up stomachs, lungs, and hearts

Exquisitely fucked up with fragile moth-eaten parts

And it's never too late to make a new start

I could make a new start at 28

At 48, at 66, 88

I know it's tough

But you are enough.
You are not wearing shoes

and carpet soft under soles of feet

You are carefree wiggles of toes in the sand

Summers first swim in the sea,

Mr Whippys!

Licking your hand as they drip down melting too quickly

You are perfectly crisp cold, and blazing beautiful heat,

you are a marvelous mess and a pocket full of neat.

You are sweets

Those white chocolate discs with the multicoloured nobbly
bobbly bits,

you are cuddles and dancing

and singing and laughing,

you are a happy accident flying high no need for a plan

You are Superman! (Superwoman)

Lost sense of sane, Weighed down by shame

Know the sunshine never feels as good as when you've just
endured a shit tonne of rain

Regaining strength, regaining fight

Happiness can be found even in the darkest of times

if one only remembers to turn on the light.

Humonculi

Written as part of Experimental Words
collaborated with Dr. Sam Gallivan

Fingers crossed

Crossed fingers

Lost tongue circle spirals in a drying mouth

Flutters

Mutters to self

Manage to find a side room that is quiet

I mistake the anxiety riot in my stomach for hunger

Adrenaline isn't enough to sustain me

Peel back the skin

Wrap fingers around the flesh of soft yellow

Swallow

Breathe

Run fingers down forearm

Feel the goosebumps and sweaty palms

I sweat a lot

Trace the scar down the back of wrist

Hands are weirdly forgiving

Held tight by control pants and an industrial sports bra

A black second scaffolding skin of lycra

Hold it all in

Looking for the wrinkles that stay

Smooth the grooves, remember the lines

Everything needs to be lines

lined up with the door else I feel disorientated

Digits dive into dark tunneled sleeves,

The nervousness unfurls into command

full bloom ...

Fingertips feel round the back

tie up the gown

A reinforced cuff of the neck

Someone else ties up knots behind

The constriction reassures me

I won't fall out

My back protected from exposure

Double knot scuffs against my skin

Numb fingers, touch thin, miss this

But you don't see me till I'm ready

I run for a last minute wee

There is always a last minute wee

We pace, my body and me, we

Pull up sleeves

Push the wall

Push the fear back

Stall the imposter

Fall back

Attempt to sit into my body,

Ground and group limbs together

Prevent them from running

No one forced our hand

Breathe deep

Stomach flips

Teeter on the edge

Heels cling to the back step

Toes grasping

Toes gasping

Accelerate of acid heart rate

Beat, beat, beat

quickening metronome

Crescendo heat radiates from beneath the bones

Pulse in fingers, red up my arms

Thumbs up

Like I'm coming up

Red neck red breast red breath

Lungs pinch and cry out sigh

Momentarily self rising and watching on from high

The inhales shake

The exhales rattle and quake

Catch breath

Cresting the wave of an orgasm

Heart beat hard heat head-butting the walls of my ribcage

The ribs are too small to encompass the breath I must harness

The first line always shakes me

The danger

The risk to see if I can do this

Sore thumb stuck out suck down
Ignore the alarms,

Reading them is easy

Ignoring them is the pro move

May I start?

Caught word in throat, cough it out

Hypersalivation

Dry mouth salvation

Spit

Spit it out then

How far would you sink if I left you asleep in the sand?

Hollow space held, the breath has left

a religious epiphany

Breathless

Two fingers tight before anyone can breathe out again

Check it holds

Hold breath between stitches

Check it holds

Skin itches with electricity

Deep lines of worry punctured with oxytocin

Pat back, clap hands, clap back

I hope I've done enough

Crossed fingers

Reassurance teeters on the edge

hand in hand with insecurity

Tugging on the ends

Fingers burned

There is no applause

Applaud the artistry

Quite a feat

Neat wounds stitched tunes back in

A desirable dexterity

Worked fingers to bone

Silence accompanies the descent back home

And I'm alone again

We're not homunculi

A little human inside a brain driving meat

We are a lived in body

We are cognition and intuition

We are ambition,

Thinking, feeling, surging and bleeding

We are difficulty in defining,

Elusive and explorable

we can't fully quantify it

We are description defying

But we're trying.

On Waking

Sunlight sneaks in from the outside eager morning
Illuminates your cheekbone
You look like an angel, glittering
radiating warmth and calm
I watch your chest rise and fall rise and fall
As a smile spreads across your face
You blink open your eyes
                   and tell me off for staring at you.

Rumpus

Hot pink legs walk out of a misunderstood mouth
and you scowl
offended by my hugging of a disco ball
I was listening
I can listen and think about dancing at the same time
The spinach is on fire
It wilts and breaks off and we're leaving a trail of
mess on our morning walk
pink legs kick
pink legs try to run away
They're not as subtle a colour as they should be
if we wanted this to be peaceful
We're playing tunes in the wrong key
and my pen burns like a cigarette
I want the glowing circles of a disco to light us home
instead we're on fire.

Here

after Adrienne Rich

There is nowhere I would rather be than here

Hear me when I say whatever happens with us, I won't ever lie.
False truths to you would burn and blister my tongue
and there are far better uses for that muscle than masochism.

Whatever happens with us, I fear that there will inevitably be
insecurity and jealousy muscle bound

waves that crash, smother, and threaten to tsunami through
the
delicate hand hold of our hearts.

I pray their clasp is stronger.

Stronger or braver

You don't have to fill the role of knight in shining armour
saviour just because of your gender.

We are bigger than the binary roles you feel instinct to fill

No yin-yang jigsaw pieces to fill, we are individually two full
circles.

We understand 'we' is made of a separate you and a separate I
to acknowledge and honour our individuality, appreciate and
celebrate that which is different, to never try to change

Or shame that which you or I are, but to love every tucked away corner, every frayed patch and hem,

Sewed together, patchwork arts with patchwork hearts.

Hearts beating faster now, Whatever happens with us our bodies will still alight on the others touch,

as if they have spent their whole existence starved, and waste no opportunity to gorge full you are

gorgeous

Trust that Whatever happens with us, I hope you will always want to listen to my stories,

always eagerly ready to step

into my tangled imagination

Even if it seemingly comes from nowhere

There is nowhere I would rather be than

here.

On Joy

like sweet
honey sticky
not overpowering
just enough
the deepest breath
full lungs stretched to their capacity
oxygen floods body
relief
peace
a piece of warm
melty peanut butter toast crunch
of multiple texture nut sticky
on roof of mouth mmm smunch
willy wonka's every flavour bubblegum
tastes like smiles
and family meals and touch and dance and laughter
breath giggle gasped for in hysteria
tears of laughter
belly ache
wheeze and howl
and sigh at the release
a furry curled up ball of oblivious calm purring
he doesn't read the news
he doesn't give a shit about instagram
marshmallows melted into the top of hot chocolate soft sweet and
easy
a mouthwash kiss before bed
satisfying
moreish

delicious
it is divine
lick your lips mmm
rub your full tummy and gratefully undo
the top button of your jeans
sigh
beat drop and tribal cry at that chorus your hormonal self fell
in love with
(that your grown up self is still in love with)
swim underwater to see rubber ducks
and fishes and mermaids blowing bubble kisses
and wishes dancing on coral colourful
seaweed dancing out of the corner of your eye
come up in jubilation break the surface
breathe
sunshine that wakes up before you
a mouthwash kiss before bed
you are divine

gulp it all down gulp it all in
smile
out at the horizon
trace out a swirled picture of secret whispers on the back

of a dozing lover snuggled under covers
spring buds greeting frost melting sprigs of hope
timeless contentment and rest
perhaps this lack of battle and effort
is your best
sourced peace
embodied pause
just for now
ust enough

Isolation

When we look back at the photo albums of these times

We alone

We selfies with our unwilling cats

We trees

We teasing out the latest bakery trend

We spread thick buttered fakery of smiles
peppering social media feed

That hungers for more than the vegan sourdough cheesecake hand
ache

We whisking more life into the banality of another day of staring at
the ceiling

Peeling off fantasies of pleasantries with strangers

In a glass clink

pint sink

cheeks pink gin wink

savoured drink

Of each others otherness

We reminisced over screen square attempts to connect

And felt emptier and more tired from the games of let's pretend

Without an end

We sighs full of rust

Clavicles coated in dust

We kissed by the sun

That reassured us all

You will rise again

Finding your feet

In a new beat of Eat/Sleep/ExistentialPanic/Cry/Eat/Sleep/Repeat

Take a seat.

      And Breeeeeathe.

Cleave at this anxious cave of chest
                        and breeeathe,
Today is just a day

Not a time limit to do list of tasks to achieve

It's ok to grieve

For those would-have-beens and might-have-beens

A summer seen in pillow planted hopes and dreams

Beamed from a heart that is cautious to start anew.

What to do?

How best to thrive?

Maybe it's ok to simply survive and get through?

You are a human. Not a robot machine who bleeds just to progress

You can rest.

Feel safe in your isolation nest.

I know it can be testing, but the best thing to remember when heart is beating toofasttooworriedtooanxioustoofast

Is to root through lost feet and comfort yourself under duvet covers of

This too shall pass.

You will rise again.

And we did and we will

Fill our glasses with laughs and hand holds and dancing bold
  to Robyn on table tops

Slot toes out of flip flops into seaside paddle pit stops on the
  way to visit everyone we know

We alone in our houses
but not in our hearts.

The ends always come with the rise of a new start.

Practice

and now I am 30
and now I am softer, heavier, less muscle and bone
but hoping I am happier
I am practising
And now I am letting my hair grow and not waxing as often as I
　　used to
I am happier
I am hoping that those 6 weeks NHS therapy was enough
I am hoping that the battle with my body is over, peace
accepted,
I am hoping I can accept her white flags and start to love her,
　　worship her in the same way that you do
and now I am hoping that 16 weeks group therapy was enough
I am worried I have reached my summit and must watch the
　　others climb ahead
I am hoping that those 16 months private therapy was enough
I am rubbing white tiger balm into my lower back because of
　　the ache
and now I am doing enough cardio to eat the food we're
　　celebrating with
without worrying
and now I am worried I'm not enough
and now I am eating vegan Ben & Jerrys without shame... most of
　　the time
I am practising
and now I am worried I haven't done enough
and now I am worried I will have wasted too much life worrying
and now I am letting him see, touch, hold all the parts of me, it

takes

practice

and now I am buying cushion covers as stress relief

And now I am investing in therapy because I know, deep down,

I am enough

and now I am in love

and now I am hoping

and now I roar

and now I am running because it feels good

I am practising

It takes practice

I am stopping wearing bras

Summer Seaside

The foreboding clouds didn't take away their sense of enjoyment
Savouring each moment
Each wave that crashed against their goose-bumped gleeful body
Each pebble picked up by curious wonderings of explorer's fingers
Each whip of the wind against rosy, weather-beaten cheeks
Each squeak of laughter and excited happy from little bodies
playing with their family
The gulls soared above them, cawing as they dived and swooped
    on the hunt for a fish and chip supper unattended
They felt mended
Wasn't it splendid to be here?
Near to the water's edge looking out on the horizon
Their eyes on out at the sheer vastness of it all
To feel so small
And so calm
And so peaceful
Their breaths slowed to the pace of the waves
It was going to be ok.

ACKNOWLEDGEMENTS

An inordinate amount of people inspired this book into existence in some way. I am endlessly thankful and feel incredibly lucky.
Here are some of them:

My best friend Lucy Lobek - who painstakingly painted this beautiful front cover, I am and will continue to be forever grateful for you darling.

For Tyrone Lewis, Dan Simpson, and Kayla Feldman who have continuously inspired and supported me in equal measure in my poetry journey and creative endeavours.

Sovereign Writers group, the sisterhood that kept me scribbling away in isolation and picked me up when I fell down- Zoe, Evie, Kayla, Hannah, Becky.

Ross Foley for unwaivering belief, encouragement, spell checks and saintly patience in letting me take over our flat to figure out the manuscript.
I love you.

Alfie who I have always aspired to be as well read and clever (and cool) as.

Alex who taught me to be funny and not take myself too seriously.

Chess who was my first fanatic reader. Who I think of whenever I'm worried about getting the words out and am instantly soothed by.

Dad, the first storyteller with the very best voices.

Mum who's always encouraged me no matter what.

Ms Richards at Dorothy Stringer who first taught me to love poetry.

Stuart at Verve, may this be the first collaboration of many. Thank you for making my dream come true.

Dear readers, may this book bring you joy, escape, adventure, but above all, comfort. Thank you for picking it up.

ABOUT VERVE POETRY PRESS

Verve Poetry Press is a quite new and already award-winning press that focused initially on meeting a local need in Birmingham - a need for the vibrant poetry scene here in Brum to find a way to present itself to the poetry world via publication. Co-founded by Stuart Bartholomew and Amerah Saleh, it now publishes poets from all corners of the UK - poets that speak to the city's varied and energetic qualities and will contribute to its many poetic stories.

Added to this is a colourful pamphlet series, many featuring poets who have performed at our sister festival - and a poetry show series which captures the magic of longer poetry performance pieces by festival alumni such as Polarbear, Matt Abbott and Genevieve Carver.

The press has been voted Most Innovative Publisher at the Saboteur Awards, and has won the Publisher's Award for Poetry Pamphlets at the Michael Marks Awards.

Like the festival, we strive to think about poetry in inclusive ways and embrace the multiplicity of approaches towards this glorious art.

www.vervepoetrypress.com
@VervePoetryPres
mail@vervepoetrypress.com